Sophocles'

Electra

Adapted by
Frank McGuinness

SAMUEL
FRENCH
FOUNDED 1830
New York Hollywood London Toronto
SAMUELFRENCH.COM

For Ann Bourke

CHARACTERS

Servant

Pylades

Orestes

Electra

Chrysothemis

Clytemnestra

Aegisthus

Chorus

Sophocles'
ELECTRA

(An old SERVANT enters with ORESTES and PYLADES.)

SERVANT.
Son of Agamemnon,
This is your father's land, the ancient city of Argos.
How long have you waited for this happy sight?
Observe it.
From here your father led the Greeks to Troy.
Here that poor demented creature, Io, wandered.
There's the market place called after Apollo.
Hera's shrine, so famous, lies to your left.
This is Mycenae,
It is beneath our feet, rich Mycenae,
Blood-red Mycenae, the murderous home of Pelops' sons.
I carried you once from this place.
Your sister snatched you from your father's corpse.
And I received you into my hands
To rear you till you were man enough
To revenge yourself against your father's murder.
That time is now, Orestes,
The hour is now,
Do it now. Decide what to do.
The day is breaking to the birds' voices.
The stars have shrunk,
The night is nothing.

Before a soul stirs out of their sleep,
Do not pause.
Decide what to do. Do it now.
     ORESTES.
Best of men,
Your loyalty shines.
A great steed may be on his last legs
But he still relishes the scent of danger.
That's the spirit in you.
Listen to me, I will tell you all,
And if I miss the mark tell me.
When I went to Delphi to ask Apollo,
How I do revenge my father's murder?
The oracle told me this.
I must use my own cunning to do the deed.
And not trust arms nor men
In the light of that oracle.
When you get a chance, go into the house,
Find out every thing they're up to.
And bring it back to me!
No one will suspect you. nor men.
Your white hair, your tired face have transformed you.
Tell them some story.
Say you are a foreigner,
You've come from Phocis, sent by Phanoteus,
He's one of their bosom pals,
And then, on your oath, you must swear—
Orestes is dead!
There was an accident—he fell from his chariot
As he raced in the games at Delphi.
Spin them that yarn.
We'll go first to my father's tomb, and honour it,
We'll spill wine and leave a lock of hair,
As Apollo ordered us to do.
We'll carry back that bronze urn, hidden in the bushes,
And entertain them with the deception

IMPORTANT BILLING AND CREDIT REQUIREMENTS

All producers of ELECTRA *must* give credit to the Author of the Play in all programs distributed in connection with performances of the Play and in all instances in which the title of the Play appears for purposes of advertising, publicizing or otherwise exploiting the Play and/or a production. The name of the Author *must* also appear on a separate line, on which no other name appears, immediately following the title, and *must* appear in size of type not less than fifty percent the size of the title type, and shall appear in the following manner:

"ELECTRA		"Sophocles'
by Sophocles	OR	ELECTRA
adapted by Frank McGuinness		adapted by Frank McGuinness"

(The following acknowledgements must also appear in all programs distributed in connection with performances of ELECTRA:)

This script of ELECTRA by Sophocles used as reference the translation of F. Storr as first published in 1912 in the Loeb Classical Library and the translation of Hugh Lloyd-Jones as published in SOPHOCLES, Vol. 1 of the Loeb Classical Library (Vol. 20). Copyright 1994 by the President and Fellows of Harvard College. Used by special arrangement with Harvard Univ. Press.

This adaptation was originally produced in the United States by McCarter Theatre, Princeton, NJ (Emily Mann, Artistic Director/Jeffrey Woodward, Managing Director) on September 18, 1998.

This new version of ELECTRA by Frank McGuinness was commissioned by the Donmar Warehouse with first performances at the Chichester Festival Theatre on September 11, 1997 and at the Donmar Warehouse Theatre on October 21, 1997.

ETHEL BARRYMORE THEATRE

🅢 A Shubert Organization Theatre

Gerald Schoenfeld, *Chairman*　　　　Philip J. Smith, *President*

Robert E. Wankel, *Executive Vice President*

ERIC KREBS	RANDALL L. WREGHITT	ANITA WAXMAN	ELIZABETH WILLIAMS	LAWRENCE HOROWITZ

present

the **McCARTER THEATRE / DONMAR WAREHOUSE** and **DUNCAN C. WELDON** production

ZOË WANAMAKER

in

SOPHOCLES'

EL*e*CTRA

Adapted by

FRANK McGUINNESS

CLAIRE BLOOM

STEPHEN SPINELLA

MICHAEL CUMPSTY

MARIN HINKLE　　DANIEL ORESKES
MIRJANA JOKOVIC　　IVAN STAMENOV
MYRA LUCRETIA TAYLOR

and

PAT CARROLL

Set and Costume Design **JOHAN ENGELS**	Lighting Design **PAUL PYANT**	Sound Design **T. RICHARD FITZGERALD**

Movement Direction **JONATHAN BUTTERELL**	Production Stage Manager **ROBERT I. COHEN**	Marketing **PRO-MARKETING**	Casting **BERNARD TELSEY CASTING**

Associate Producers **MARCIA ROBERTS LAUREN DOLL JUNE CURTIS LYNNE PEYSER**	Press Representative **JAMES LL MORRISON**	Production Supervisor **LARRY MORLEY**	General Management **EKTM: ERIC KREBS/ JONATHAN SHULMAN**

Directed by

DAVID LEVEAUX

This new version by Frank McGuinness, commissioned by the Donmar Warehouse, opened at the Chichester Festival Theatre on September 11, 1997, at the Donmar Warehouse Theatre on October 21, 1997 and on September 18, 1998 at McCarter Theatre, Princeton, NJ, Emily Mann, Artistic Director/Jeffrey Woodward, Managing Director.

The Producers wish to express their appreciation to Theatre Development Fund for its support of this production.

That I am burnt to ashes.
Will that bring bad luck?
So what if the word is I am dead,
When the truth is I am safe and sound,
Ready to earn my fame.
Words used to your advantage can't bring bad.
I've heard of heroes in the past,
They were presumed dead and when they rose again,
The honour given to them was all the greater.
The rumour of my sad story will do just that.
I will blaze like a meteor through my enemies.
But grant me good luck, you, my home.
My father's house,
My father's land.
My father's gods.
For those same gods have hastened me here
To scrub you clean of stain.
Don't let me be dishonoured,
Don't send me from this land.
Let me prosper,
Let me put this house back on its feet.
I have said enough.
Old man, do what you have to do.
We will do the same.
The time's come, and no man cheats time.

(ELECTRA howls from within.)

    SERVANT.
Some servant woman is crying inside.
    ORESTES.
Electra—could it be her weeping?
Could we stay and hear what breaks her heart?
    SERVANT
We could not.
You do what Apollo demands, he is a god.

He knows what we should do.
Pour wine on your father's grave.
Agamemnon. His tomb.
He will help us.
And we'll succeed. We will succeed.

(SERVANT and ORESTES exit.
ELECTRA enters from the palace, chanting.)

ELECTRA.
Divine light,
Sweet air,
Again hear
My pain.
Divine light,
Sweet air,
Again hear
My pain.
Have you not witnessed when morning breaks
My heart break, my heart break?
When night falls, I do not feast
In this house of ghosts.
I lie alone.
My father's dead.
He did not die in war.
He does not lie on a foreign shore.
Here, at home,
My mother's hands turned red
With his blood. Adulteress,
Adulterer, she and Aegisthus,
Split him open with an axe.
The tree fell,
And father, I am left to dwell
Alone in your house, my back
Against the wall,
Weeping for my father dead,

Mourning my dead father.
But I swear, while my eyes see
The sun or stars in the sky,
I will never cease to cry out
My pain and my complaint.
I will be like the poor nightingale
Who killed her young,
Then sorrow raped her heart.
That is the song I will spill
Through this house where blood was spilt.
I call upon Persephone,
I call upon the dead,
I call upon the Furies,
Revenge my father's blood-stained marriage bed,
Revenge my father,
Send me back my brother,
I can no longer stomach the size of my sorrow.

(The CHORUS enters.)

    CHORUS.
Electra, child, you're wasting away with grief.
Because your mother's heartless, you're left to mourn the cruel
       fate of your father.
She betrayed him, and her lover knifed him.
A dirty death's in store for sinners of that nature.
May the gods forgive me saying it.
    ELECTRA.
You're good people. You've come to comfort me.
I do know you have kind hearts.
But you should know I have a job to do,
And that is to weep sore tears over my dead father.
You pay kindness back with kindness, you're my friends,
So I beg you, leave me be, leave me.
    CHORUS.
Your father is dead.

You can't cry him back from his grave.
Your prayers can't raise him up again.
You will die from all this grieving.
Will you not rest from it, when it will bring you no remedy?
It is pointless—why do you persist?
    ELECTRA.
It's a cruel child that forgets a father's cruel end.
I'd sooner turn to stone and my tears into rivers.
    CHORUS.
You're not alone in your sorrow—others share your burden.
Your sisters Iphianassa and Chrysothemis.
They feel their affliction too. Think of them.
Think of your brother in his sorrow,
A young man far from his home.
Heaven send him here to us soon, Orestes;
He'll make Mycenae his own, he'll take his father's throne.
    ELECTRA.
I've waited for him long years,
Crying barren spinsters' tears.
I'm drenched lamenting my fate.
The many wrongs we've suffered.
He knows them all—not a word.
I hear he dreams he'll come home.
It's buried deep in his bones.
Aye, let him dream, we must wait.
    CHORUS.
Keep your strength, girl, have strength.
God is still great in his heaven, and he sees everything.
Offer up to him what is eating you inside.
Don't go on fire with hatred.
Remember this—time's a gentle god, he heals.
Agamemnon's son may wander the plains of Crisa,
But he will not forget his father,
And the God of Death will not forget either.
    ELECTRA.
The best days of my life are finished.

I have neither hope nor strength.
I'm a childless woman who is melting away.
I have no man to protect me.
I live like a slave in my father's house.
I dress like a beggar—eat what's thrown me.
    CHORUS.
A terrible cry greeted your father home,
And he gave a terrible cry in return.
The blow of the axe cut him in two.
They were as cunning as they were passionate,
And they did the deed. Where did it spring from?
This filthy act—was it God or man?
    ELECTRA.
That cursed day, that sorest night,
At the feast to welcome him home
They cut my father like meat.
They laid their hands upon him.
They took his life, took my life.
Great God in heaven, hear me.
Make them suffer, make them weep.
May their power turn to nothing.
May they die and turn to nothing.
    CHORUS.
Hold your tongue.
Has it never dawned on you how much you make your own
        misery?
You pile on your agony.
You're a feeble woman fighting mighty enemies.
    ELECTRA.
I have harmed myself by the harm done to me.
I know the hardness of my heart.
But as long as there is breath left in my body,
I will not change direction no matter how harmful.
Dear sisters if you admit the truth,
What word of comfort could console me?
There is no end to my lamenting.

There never will be an end to my sorrow.
    CHORUS.
Well don't add sorrow on to sorrow.
I'm speaking as a friend, a mother you can trust.
    ELECTRA.
I have harmed myself by the harm done to me.
I know the hardness of my heart.
But as long as there is breath left in my body,
I will not change direction no matter how harmful.
Dear sisters if you admit the truth,
What word of comfort could console me?
There is no end to lamenting.
There never will be an end to my sorrow.
    CHORUS.
Well don't add sorrow on to sorrow.
I'm speaking as a friend, a mother you can trust.
    ELECTRA.
What limit is there to what torments me?
Tell me, is it an honour to forget the dead?
Is it in the nature of the living to do that?
If there are such people, may they scorn me.
And if I possess anything good that I value,
May I lose it if I stop this mourning,
If I dishonour—if I forget my father.
If a dead man is to turn to dirt and nothing,
And those who did it do not pay the wages of their sin,
If they themselves are not murdered in return,
Then the gods are dead and there is no faith.
    CHORUS.
I'm thinking in my own interest as much as your, daughter.
If I am wrong, have it your own way.
We will never leave you.
    ELECTRA.
Women, I am ashamed if I upset you with all this weeping.
Forgive me, I have to do it, I have to.
Could any woman with good blood in her veins do otherwise?

I see the suffering in my father's house.
I see that suffering day and night.
It gets worse, not better.
First, look at myself and the mother who bore me—
I hate her.
Then look at me living in my own home with my father's
          killers.
They rule me.
They decide if I get or I go without.
How do you think I survive the days when I see him,
I see Aegisthus sitting on my father's throne?
He wears every stitch my father wore.
He pours wine on the same fire where he murdered.
And the worst—what is worse—
I see my father's bed, and his killer lies beside my mother.
Mother—is that a fit name for such a woman?
She is so depraved she lives with that obscenity.
She fears no force of retribution.
It's as if she's gloating over what she's done.
She celebrates the date her treachery killed my father.
Cattle are slaughtered, and they dance.
Every month she gives sacrifice to the gods that protect her.
And I am the unfortunate woman, alone in the house,
Lamenting, wasting away, looking at this abomination,
Weeping at the feast they call after my father.
And I am not allowed to cry my heart's content.
That gracious woman gives full vent to her insulting tongue.
'You are full of hate, girl, you're accursed.
Have you and you alone lost a father?
Has no one else ever known grief?
May your death be sore and the gods damn you.'
That's how she insults me, and then she hears Orestes will
          return.
She works herself into a thundering rage, she roars,
'You are the cause of this, aren't you?
You stole Orestes from my arms, you smuggled him away,

You will pay the hard price you deserve.'
She's foaming these words like a mad dog,
And her noble husband stands urging her on,
That complete coward, that deadly scourge,
A man letting his woman fight his battles.
And I will turn to dust waiting for Orestes;
Come back, put an end to this, or I will die in misery.
I hear he's coming, then he does not come,
And so he's destroyed whatever hope I dared hope.
My friends, that is how I lead my life.
There's nothing holy anymore, nothing sane nor sensible.
The world's turned bad, and so have I.
    CHORUS.
Tell me, are you saying this when Aegisthus is in the house?
Is he away from home?
    ELECTRA.
Of course he's away.
I would not set foot outside the door if he were inside.
He is in the country.
    CHORUS.
If that's so, I'd press you further.
    ELECTRA.
It's so. Ask what you want to ask.
    CHORUS.
Your brother—will he come or not?
I want to know.
    ELECTRA.
He says that he will come.
He does none of the things he says he will do.
    CHORUS.
A man takes his time when he's to do a great deed.
    ELECTRA.
I did not take my time when I saved him.
    CHORUS.
You know his heart is good—he will help his friends.

ELECTRA.
I believe it, or else I could not stay alive.
   CHORUS.
Say no more for I see your sister, Chrysothemis,
Your full sister from the same father and same mother.
She's carrying offerings from the house to give to the dead.

(CHRYSOTHEMIS enters.)

   CHRYSOTHEMIS.
What are the things you are saying outside the house, sister?
After so long lamenting, will you not learn you are wasting
       your time?
Your anger's useless.
I know well enough, how bad our way of life is.
I also know what my feelings are.
If I'd power, I'd tell our masters.
But these are dangerous waters and we must move carefully.
Nothing I do must threaten them.
I want you to do the same.
I know you have justice on your side, and I do not.
But they have power.
I must obey them in everything if I'm to be a free woman.
   ELECTRA.
You are your father's daughter, and you should be ashamed.
You forget him because you respect your mother.
You lecture me with what you learnt from her.
You do not have a word to say for yourself.
You make your choice.
You be foolish, like me, or you be wise and forget your own.
You said if you had power they would feel your hatred.
You then betray me when I do all I can to honour my father.
You try to stop me.
You'd be a coward as well as a victim, would you?
You teach me or you listen to me:
What would it profit me to stop mourning?

Do I not have a life?
A miserable life, but it is enough for me.
And if I harm them, then it is an honour,
A pleasure for the dead if the dead feel pleasure.
You say that you hate them, but it's only a word, your hatred.
You live among them, you live with your father's killers.
Well, the earth will cover me before I give in to them,
Not if they were to give me your pomp and your pleasures.
You eat yourself full and your life is a leisure.
What I eat does not sicken my stomach.
I have no desire to enjoy your privilege.
You would not either if you were thinking rightly.
You could be called the daughter of the greatest of men.
You choose, as things stand, to be your mother's child.
You are what you seem to be—a traitor.
You have betrayed your dead father.
You have betrayed your own.
    CHORUS.
Please, say nothing in anger.
There's wisdom on both sides.
Learn from her, and she learns from you.
    CHRYSOTHEMIS.
I've grown used to her way of talking.
I would not have broken breath but that I did learn something.
She is facing great danger.
That will put a stop to her lamenting.
    ELECTRA.
Great danger—what is it? Come on, tell me.
If it's worse that what I now endure, I will not say another
        word.
    CHRYSOTHEMIS.
Then I'll tell you all I know.
They will lock you away from the light of the sun if you don't
        stop lamenting.
You will be taken away from this country.
You will be buried alive in a dungeon and left to mourn there.

Take stock of that, and don't blame me afterwards.
You have the chance to show some sense.
    ELECTRA.
They have decided to do that to me?
    CHRYSOTHEMIS.
When Aegisthus comes home, yes.
    ELECTRA.
Then let him come home soon.
    CHRYSOTHEMIS.
You are crazed—what curse are you putting on yourself?
    ELECTRA.
Let him come, if these things you say he has in mind—
    CHRYSOTHEMIS.
May happen to you? What kind of madness makes you want—
    ELECTRA.
To get away as far as possible from you all.
    CHRYSOTHEMIS.
You do not care to leave the life you lead now?
    ELECTRA.
Yes, the life I lead now is wonderfully agreeable.
    CHRYSOTHEMIS.
It would be, if you had some logic—
    ELECTRA.
And is it your logic to be disloyal to my own?
Is that what you teach me?
    CHRYSOTHEMIS.
I am not trying to teach you that, but to bow the knee to those
        in power.
    ELECTRA.
You can bow the knee, I will stand upright.
    CHRYSOTHEMIS.
Honour demands you do not come to grief through being
        stubborn and stupid.
    ELECTRA.
My father's honour, I will defend, and if I must, I will come
        to grief.

CHRYSOTHEMIS.
But our father does not demand this. He will forgive us this—
          I know.
ELECTRA.
The words of a coward, and you said them.
CHRYSOTHEMIS.
Will you not stand with me and say them too?
ELECTRA.
No. I am not so stupid.
CHRYSOTHEMIS.
Then I will go about my own business.
ELECTRA.
Where are you going? Why are you carrying those offerings?
CHRYSOTHEMIS.
For my father's grave—my mother sent me with them.
ELECTRA.
What are you saying?
She's making offerings at the grave of her worst enemy?
CHRYSOTHEMIS.
To the man she murdered, is that what you mean?
ELECTRA.
Who persuaded her to do this? Who approved of this?
CHRYSOTHEMIS.
I believe she had a terrible dream.
ELECTRA.
My father and my father's father, may your gods help me
          at last.
CHRYSOTHEMIS.
Do you find some hope in her terror?
ELECTRA.
I can tell you that if you can tell me about her dream.
CHRYSOTHEMIS.
I know very little.
ELECTRA.
Tell me.
Very little may be enough to swing fate in our favour.

CHRYSOTHEMIS.
They say our father came back to life.
He returned to the light of day.
The sceptre he used to carry, the one Aegisthus carries now.
My father took it and planted it beside the fire.
It grew into a bough thick with fruit.
It cast its shadow over all Mycenae.
She told her dream to the Sun.
Someone near her heard and told me this story.
It is her fear makes her send me to the grave.
I know no more.
I beg you, by all the gods we believe in, do as I say.
Stop this foolishness or you'll come to great harm.
If you cast me aside, you'll come to me regretting it.

ELECTRA.
My dear sister, leave nothing on the tomb.
That woman hated our father.
Neither God nor man would let her honour his grave.
Give them to the wind.
Hide them deep in the dust.
They won't disturb where my father lies dead.
Save them for herself when death takes her.
She is so without shame she dares to pray for the man she
              murdered.
Do you think the man dead in the earth will receive her
              offerings?
She dishonoured him in death.
She killed him like an enemy.
She cut his corpse to ribbons.
And she wiped the blood off her hands on his head.
Do you believe these offerings will clear her of the murder?
That cannot be.
Get rid of them.
Go to our father's grave and cut a lock from your hair.
Take this tangled one from my unhappy head.
It's very little, but it's all I have.

My belt too, it's a poor thing, but give them to him.
Kneel and pray that in his kindness,
He comes from beneath and helps us scatter our enemies.
Pray that he'll come and destroy all who stand against us.
Someday we may make him richer offerings than they do now.
I do believe—I truly believe this—
He sent these terrible dreams to her.
Sister, do this and you will help us both.
You will help the most loved of all men.
Our father, our dead father.
       CHORUS.
Her words are holy.
Dear girl, if you're wise, do as she says.
       CHRYSOTHEMIS.
It's my duty, I'll do it.
There will be no argument.
But if you care about me, good women,
Say nothing about what I'm doing.
If my mother hears of it, it will be on my head.

(CHRYSOTHEMIS exits.)

       CHORUS.
May I not bear false witness,
But through the darkness,
I see the workings of Justice.
She knows what has to be.
She will plant her fatal kiss
On the lips of your enemies.
And soon she will be here.
My mind is dancing.
That dream's destroyed my fears.
I heard that and my heart took wing.
Your father, leader of the Greeks,
He will always remember,
And the axe that bloodied his brave cheek

Waits the call from its bronze lair.
Bronze too are the terrible claws
Of the god who devours the lawless.
She has seen the bed where adulterers sleep,
Seen the wedding clothes, the wedding feast,
And her gift will be a pit so deep
No cry of comfort from man nor beast
Shall reach their ears who did the deed
And sinned against the mighty gods.
It's clear as day for all to read
Revenge will never spare the rod.
If there's no truth in that woman's dream,
Our prayers are lost and dying screams.
The founder of this house,
Pelops, long ago,
You began this sorrow.
Thrown from his chariot,
Martilus died, brought
Down by your deceit,
And sorrows meet
With sorrow since in this unhappy house.

(CLYTEMNESTRA enters.)

   CLYTEMNESTRA.
So you're prowling outside the house again,
It's easy seeing Aegisthus is not here.
At least he stops you shaming your family in the eye of the
          world.
Now he's away and you show me no respect.
Your constant refrain is that I'm cruel,
That I do great harm to you and yours.
I am not a cruel woman.
But I do abuse you because you abuse me so often.
And your excuse is your father, nothing else.
I killed him.

I know it well.
I do not deny it.
But I did not act alone.
Justice killed him too.
If you'd come to your senses, you would be on her side.
Tell me, this father of yours that you're constantly lamenting,
Tell me why he and he alone among the Greeks,
Why did he sacrifice your sister to the gods?
His child that he had the pleasure to conceive—
I had the pain to give her birth.
Tell me why he did this, explain.
For whose sake did he sacrifice her?
For the Greeks, would you say?
But they have no right to kill her.
She was mine. My child.
And if it was for his brother, Menelaus, that he killed her,
Should he not have paid the penalty to me?
He cut her soft white throat, my Iphigenia. My child.
If I had touched Orestes, he would have killed me.
He killed my daughter—why should he not die?
Menelaus had two children.
They ought to have died, not mine.
Was it not for their father and mother that this war started?
Did death want to grow fat on my children, not hers?
Did your damned father feel pity for the children of Menelaus?
Had he no pity for mine?
I killed him—I made the only choice I could.
Your father was a fool, he was insane.
That's what she would say, if she could still speak,
My dead daughter.
And I do not regret what was done.
And were you dead, you would have demanded I did the deed.
Before you judge me, judge yourself.
Are you so sure of the ground you stand on?

ELECTRA.
This time, don't accuse me of starting the quarrel.
But if you deign to listen, I want to tell the truth,
The truth about my father and my sister.
CLYTEMNESTRA.
I allow that.
If you had always spoken so civilly, I would have listened
more to you.
ELECTRA.
Then listen now.
You say that you killed my father.
Whether you acted justly or not, what greater crime could you
admit to?
And I tell you that you did not kill him in the name of Justice.
You acted under the influence of an evil man.
And you are now living with him.
Ask Artemis, the goddess of the hunt, why she stilled the
winds in Aulis?
No, let me tell you, because we cannot question her. She is
a goddess.
They say my father was hunting in a grove sacred to the
divinity.
He startled a deer, a dappled, horned stag.
When he killed the animal, she heard him boasting,
And in her anger, Artemis detained our ships.
A sacrifice had to be made: his daughter for the beast.
That is how she went to her death.
There was no other way for the army to go home or get to
Troy.
That is why he sacrificed her.
It was against his will, and with great suffering.
It was not done for the sake of Menelaus.
But say you're right, say he had done it to help him,
Was that a reason for him to die at your hands?
Whose law is that?
You watch when you lay down the law.

You may be laying down your own pain and punishment.
If you were to get what you deserve,
If we are to take a life for a life,
You should die first.
The excuse you make for yourself does not excuse you.
Tell me this.
Why are you bedding the man who killed my father?
He is guilty.
You give him children.
You cast aside your older children—
We fear God because our father feared God,
So I do not excuse your adultery.
Or do you say that too is for your dead daughter?
If you do, then it is beyond shame.
You sleep with a dire enemy for your daughter's sake.
I'm wasting my breath talking to you.
You say all I do is abuse my mother.
Mother.
No—you torture me.
You torture us all.
I lead an unhappy life.
I live with the constant cruelty you and your mate pour on me.
And another child wears himself away in exile.
Orestes.
He barely escaped from your bloodstained hands.
You've often accused me that I saved him to make you suffer.
Well, know this.
If I'd had the power, I would have done so.
Tell that to the world.
If you think me wicked, arrogant, shameless—good.
That proves me worthy to be your breed.
    CHORUS.
There's a fire in her head.
It's burning her up. She's not just.
She doesn't care what she's saying.

CLYTEMNESTRA.

What should I care about her? She has so insulted her mother.
She's a grown woman.
Will she stop at nothing—has she no shame?

ELECTRA.

Yes, I do feel shame, even if you might not think so.
I know what I'm doing's wrong—
It goes against my nature.
But you are malign, you are cruel.
You force me to act against my will.
And if I shock you, you've taught me how to.

CLYTEMNESTRA.

You are a disgrace.
All I say and do gives you more ammunition.

ELECTRA.

All you say, all you do is your doing and saying.
You find the words fit for what you do.

CLYTEMNESTRA.

I swear by Artemis you will face Aegisthus when he's home.

ELECTRA.

Please, offer your sacrifice.
Don't let me stop you.
I will say no more.

CLYTEMNESTRA.

Raise up my offerings of the fruits of the earth.
I pray to the Lord to lift my terrible fears.
Phoebus Apollo, my protector, listen to my heart's secret.
I am not among friends.
I cannot speak openly while she stands near me.
Her hatred and bitter words would spread lies through the
          city.
Listen to me, and hear my secret.
Great Apollo, two visions came in dreams last night.
If they bode well, fulfil them.
But if they are bad omens, turn them against my enemies.

If some plan to rob me of the wealth I possess, prevent them.
Let me live a life unharmed.
Let me rule the house of Atreus and this kingdom.
Let me live among friends.
Let my days be prosperous.
Let the children who wish me no pain prosper too.
God Apollo, hear me kindly.
Give to me and mine what we pray for.
There is more that I want, but cannot say.
You are a god, and you know well what it is.
The children of Zeus see everything.

(An old SERVANT enters.)

    SERVANT.
Women of Mycenae, is this the house of Aegisthus?
    CHORUS.
It is, stranger, you've guessed right.
    SERVANT.
Am I right to guess this lady is his wife?
She has the look of a queen.
    CHORUS.
That is the very lady.
    SERVANT.
Great lady, I bring good news from a friend to you and
        Aegisthus.
    CLYTEMNESTRA.
I welcome you, but want to know who sent you?
    SERVANT.
Phanoteus, and it concerns an important matter.
    CLYTEMNESTRA.
You come from a friend and your words will be friendly.
What is this important matter?
    SERVANT.
Orestes is dead.

(ELECTRA howls.)

CLYTEMNESTRA.
What are you saying?
Pay no heed to her.
What are you saying, stranger?
SERVANT.
I said, Orestes is dead. I say—
ELECTRA.
Orestes is dead, and I am no more.
CLYTEMNESTRA.
Be quiet.
Are you telling me the truth, stranger?
How did he die?
SERVANT.
That is what I've come to tell you.
He came with the pride of Greece to the Delphic Games.
When the first race was proclaimed he entered—
A magnificent man, admired by all eyes.
He ran as well as he looked, he won the great prize.
No other man enjoyed such triumphs—
He won victory in each and every contest.
Great cheers went to heaven,
Orestes, the Greek, has won.
The son of Agamemnon, the leader against Troy.
That's how things went, but if the gods are up to badness,
Even the mightiest man will fall.
The next day, at sunrise, the chariots would race.
He entered the lists with many others.
The first was an Achaen, the second a Spartan,
Two came from Libyan, skilled charioteers.
Orestes came next, his mares from Thessaly.
The sixth, with chestnut colts, hailed from Aetolia.
The seventh was Magnesian, and the eighth, an Aenian, had
          white horses.

The ninth came from Athens, built by the gods,
And the last was Boeotian, filling the tenth chariot.
The umpires drew lots and signed each his place.
The brazen trumpets sound, and the chariots start.
The reins are tight, the steeds are ready, they shout,
And the whole course is the clash of rattling chariots.
The dust is rising, and they nearly collide.
For each man goaded on the creatures before him;
Each wished to pass the wheels and the others' panting steeds.
The horses' breath has turned to foam,
They drenched the drivers' backs and wheels.
Orestes kept his horses near the pillar,
He grazed the post, he checked his pursuer.
And so it continues, they are all unscathed,
But beware the milk-white hard-mouthed Aenian steeds,
They bolt between the sixth and seventh round,
They dash their brains against the Barcaean chariot.
One driver crashes into another's path,
And the wreckage covers the whole plain of Crisa.
The driver from Athens, he knows his stuff,
He slackens, stops, he draws aside,
The surge of chariots in complete confusion.
Orestes stays in the rear, he's trusting in the finish,
He sees the Athenian alone is left,
He gives a roar to the racing horses, they rush on,
They bring their chariots together, they're level,
First one, then the other is in front.
Orestes kept his nerve, the horses kept on course,
Then, as the horses turned, his left hand relaxed,
Before he knew it he struck the pillar's edge.
The axle box breaks, he slides over the rail,
He falls to the ground, the horses mad in the middle of the
          course.
And a cry of pity rises for the young man,
So brave and so bloody his end,
Flung to the earth, his feet soaring to the sky.

The drivers with great difficulty stopped their horses.
They free his corpse—no friend would know him,
disfigured, dirty with blood.
They buried him on a funeral pyre, the Phoceans.
This magnificent man, now miserable dust,
They poured into an urn to carry to his home.
That is the terrible story I have to tell you.
For those who saw it with their own eyes,
There was never a sadder sight.

    CHORUS.

Our ancient house is over, destroyed root and branch.

    CLYTEMNESTRA.

Oh God, what is this?
Is it fortunate or terrible?
Do I gain from it?
It troubles me that I keep my life through my great loss.

    SERVANT.

Lady, why are you downhearted at my news?

    CLYTEMNESTRA.

Giving birth is strange.
You do not hate your children, no matter how they treat you.

    SERVANT.

Then my coming here was in vain.

    CLYTEMNESTRA.

No, not in vain—do not say in vain.
Do you have proof that he is dead,
The son I gave birth to?
I nurtured him at my breast, but in exile he turned from me.
He left this land and never saw me,
He blamed me for his father's murder,
He swore revenge against me.
Sweet sleep never closed my eyes day nor night since,
I live like a woman condemned to die.
This day I have been freed from fear,
The fear of him and that woman there.
She was a worse torture.

She lived in my house, draining my life blood,
But now I'll pass my days in peace for all her threats.
    ELECTRA.
Orestes!
I can lament your fate.
Your mother mocks it.
Am I not well off?
    CLYTEMNESTRA.
No, but he is, where he is.
    ELECTRA.
Nemesis, Goddess of Revenge, hear what she's said of
        her son.
    CLYTEMNESTRA.
Nemesis has heard what she needed to hear.
She's made up her own mind.
    ELECTRA.
Mock me—You are the winner in this.
    CLYTEMNESTRA.
Then will you and Orestes put a stop to this?
    ELECTRA.
It's we who have been stopped, not us stopping you.
    CLYTEMNESTRA.
Stranger, if you had silenced that roaring mouth,
You would have been well rewarded.
    SERVANT.
If all is well, then may I leave?
    CLYTEMNESTRA.
No, you deserve a better welcome.
Come in, leave her to lament.
She and her friends have plenty to cry over.

(CLYTEMNESTRA and the SERVANT enter the palace.)

    ELECTRA.
Do you think that creature weeps for her son in pain and
        grief?

No, she is gloating.
Orestes!
Orestes, by your death I die as well.
I have lost my last hope.
You would come and revenge my father and myself.
Now where can I go?
I have lost you and my father.
Now I must serve those I hate most,
The murderers of my father.
Do you call that justice?
No, I'll never darken their door again.
I'll walk out that gate and die alone.
If they loathe me, let them kill me.
To die would be a pleasure, to survive would be pain—
I have no wish to live.
    CHORUS.
Zeus, where are your bolts of thunder?
Where is the fire of the sun?
Can they look now and not see this?

(ELECTRA howls in pain.)

Daughter, do not cry.

(ELECTRA howls again.)

Do not weep so loudly.
    ELECTRA.
You are tearing my heart in two.
    CHORUS.
How do we do that?
    ELECTRA.
Don't breathe a word of hope that he who's dead is
        still alive.
Do that and you dance on my breaking heart.

CHORUS.
A woman's golden necklace brought down King Amphiaraus,
And now beneath the earth—
    ELECTRA.
This pain—
    CHORUS.
He lives, warm and well—
    ELECTRA.
Great pain—
    CHORUS.
Great pain came to her—her—
    ELECTRA.
His killer!
    CHORUS.
Yes.
    ELECTRA.
I know, I know.
But Amphiaraus had his champion.
I too had one, now snatched from me.
    CHORUS.
Your heart is sore, so is your fate.
    ELECTRA.
I know that too well.
My life is a river.
It floods with grief.
And it never stops, this flood.
    CHORUS.
We have watched your tears fall.
    ELECTRA.
Then let them still fall.
Give me no hope nor comfort.
My brother is dead.
    CHORUS.
All men die.

ELECTRA.
To die as he did, a poor young man?
Tangled in the reins, beneath the horse's brutal hooves?
    CHORUS.
Do not think of the horror.
    ELECTRA.
To die among strangers—I could not touch him—

(The CHORUS howls with pain.)

He was put in the earth.
We gave him no funeral.
We shed no tears over him.

(CHRYSOTHEMIS enters.)

    CHRYSOTHEMIS.
Dear sister, I raced here to give you great news.
It will bring an end to all your suffering.
    ELECTRA.
An end to all my suffering?
There is neither relief nor remedy.
    CHRYSOTHEMIS.
Orestes is here—
Do you know what I'm saying?
Orestes is here, just as I am here.
    ELECTRA.
Sister, are you mad?
Are you mocking me and yourself?
    CHRYSOTHEMIS.
I swear by my father I'm not mocking.
I'm telling you we have him here.
    ELECTRA.
No, it's not so.
Who has told you this story that you believe so easily?

CHRYSOTHEMIS.
I believe it because I saw the signs with my own eyes.
I didn't hear it from another soul.
    ELECTRA.
What have you seen that proves it?
What evidence have you?
What madness is in your mind?
    CHRYSOTHEMIS.
Listen and learn from me, than say if I'm mad.
    ELECTRA.
Speak on, if that will please you.
    CHRYSOTHEMIS.
Then I'll tell you all I saw.
I approached my father's grave, there were streams of milk
        flowing,,
And round the urn a garland of every kind of flower.
I was astounded, and looked about me.
Was someone watching?
Nothing stirred, no one, so I crept nearer the tomb,
And there at the grave's edge—a fresh-cut lock of hair.
And my soul knew—it saw Orestes.
Orestes!
An omen, a sign from the one I love most in this world.
I took it in my hands, I couldn't speak,
My eyes were crying tears of joy.
I knew it then, I knew for certain.
This precious offering was his.
Who else but you or me could put it there?
I swear to you, it was not my doing, nor yours.
How could it be you?
You cannot leave the house even to worship.
Was it our mother then?
That is not her way.
And she could not have done it without us noticing.
It is Orestes.
These offerings at the tomb came from him.

Dear sister, have courage.
We are not always victims of the same fate.
We've had our share of bad fortune.
Maybe today it's turning to good.
    ELECTRA.
Good girl, I pity your innocent wit.
    CHRYSOTHEMIS.
Is my news not good news?
    ELECTRA.
You're living in the land of dreams, and you don't know it.
    CHRYSOTHEMIS.
How can I not know what I saw with my two eyes?
    ELECTRA.
He is dead, my poor girl.
Don't look to a dead man for salvation.
That chance is gone.
    CHRYSOTHEMIS.
No.
Who told you this?
    ELECTRA.
From a man who saw him meet his fate.
    CHRYSOTHEMIS.
What man—where?
I cannot fathom this.
    ELECTRA.
He is inside with our mother.
Her welcome was not cold.
    CHRYSOTHEMIS.
No—no.
Who left the wreathes—who poured the milk on to the grave?
    ELECTRA.
Someone kind has left offerings to our dead Orestes.
    CHRYSOTHEMIS.
And I was the poor fool rushing here with good news.
I did not know our pitiful plight.
Now I find new sorrows added to our old.

ELECTRA.
That is how things stand.
Listen to me now.
You will lighten the load of the burden we carry.
    CHRYSOTHEMIS.
How can I make the dead rise?
    ELECTRA.
That is not what I said—I am not insane.
    CHRYSOTHEMIS.
Then what can I do—what are you asking?
    ELECTRA.
You must bring yourself to do what I advise.
    CHRYSOTHEMIS.
If I can do it, I will.
    ELECTRA.
Remember—to succeed you must put your shoulder to the
        work.
    CHRYSOTHEMIS.
I know that, and I'll use all my strength.
    ELECTRA.
Then listen to what I am determined to do.
You know as well as I do we've no friends here.
Death has robbed us blind, we two are alone.
While my brother lived and prospered, I had hopes.
He would appear and avenge his father.
Now that he's dead, I'm turning to you.
You are my sister, I need a sister's help.
We must murder—don't back away—
We must murder our father's murderer.
Kill Aegisthus.
Now I've spelt it out for you.
Why hesitate?
What hope have you to look forward to?
You have been cheated of your inheritance.
Will you watch you life withering away?
Will you live unloved, with no wedding bed?

Don't dream married bliss is in store for you.
Aegisthus is not that stupid a man.
He won't risk his destruction form your child or mine.
Take my advice and you will profit handsomely.
Your name, to our dead father, our brother too,
You name will be holy to them.
You will show yourself to be a free-born woman.
You will marry well—
A worthy woman delights all men.
Consent—
Do you see the honour together we will win?
What friend or stranger will not greet us with praise?
They'll cry, 'Look at the two sisters!
They saved their father's house.
They looked their enemy in the eye,
They avenged murder.
Love them, revere them,
At every feast honour their bravery.'
Our name will be celebrated far and wide,
Our glory will live after death.
Sweet sister, work with your father,
Side with your brother,
Save me from my sorrows and save yourself.
Remember this.
Shame is truly shame to a noble soul.
        CHORUS.
In matters like these it's wise to be cautious—
Both of you, be cautious.
        CHRYSOTHEMIS.
If she had an ounce of sense in her, before she opened her
            mouth,
She would have exercised caution but, good women, she
            doesn't.
Just who do you imagine that you are—
Full of fighting talk and I'm to follow you?
You are a woman, not a man—do you know that?

You are no match against those against you.
They have the good fortune, we the bad.
They're on the rise and we are sinking.
Who would battle with such a mighty man?
If you do, you will be eaten without salt.
If anyone's heard your words, we're in deeper trouble.
What good is glory? If we die in disgrace?
Dying is easy—
But locked up longing for death, and being denied it,
That is beyond shame.
I beg you , before we wreck ourselves entirely,
Restrain your anger.
All you've said to me will be breath wasted.
You are powerless, they have power, learn to give in.
    CHORUS.
Listen to her, Electra.
Think of the future, go easy, you must.
    ELECTRA.
Just as I imagined.
Before you opened your mouth I knew you'd turn your
        back.
I'll stand alone and I myself will do it.
Though I'm on my own, it will be done, because it must be.
    CHRYSOTHEMIS.
Good for you.
It's a pity you weren't so determined when father died.
What would you have done then?
    ELECTRA.
My spirit was the same, but my head was not ready.
    CHRYSOTHEMIS.
Try to keep that head on your shoulders still.
    ELECTRA.
I take it you refuse to help me?
    CHRYSOTHEMIS.
I do, because you will fail.

ELECTRA.
You're wise, well done—you're a coward, damn you.
CHRYSOTHEMIS.
You condemn me now, you'll praise me later,
I'll listen to them one and the same.
ELECTRA.
You'll never listen to praise from me.
CHRYSOTHEMIS.
Time will tell—we'll see.
ELECTRA.
Get from my sight—you're useless to me.
CHRYSOTHEMIS.
Useless I'm not—but you won't listen or learn.
ELECTRA.
Run to your mother—tell her all about it.
CHRYSOTHEMIS.
I do not hate you that much.
ELECTRA.
But you do not respect me, I know.
CHRYSOTHEMIS.
Not respect you? I want to help you.
ELECTRA.
So you decide what is right and wrong?
CHRYSOTHEMIS.
When you return to reason, I'll follow you.
ELECTRA.
Very wise you are, and very wrong.
CHRYSOTHEMIS.
My words to you exactly.
ELECTRA.
Do you not think what I say is right?
CHRYSOTHEMIS.
Sometimes being right is wrong.
ELECTRA.
I will not live with such a lie.

CHRYSOTHEMIS.
If you do this, you'll see that I was right.
ELECTRA.
I will do it, and I won't be swayed by you.
CHRYSOTHEMIS.
Is that really so—will you not think again?
ELECTRA.
No—nothing is worse than wrong advice.
CHRYSOTHEMIS.
You're deaf to every word I argue.
ELECTRA.
I decided this long ago.
CHRYSOTHEMIS.
I'll leave you to it.
My words won't turn you from your ways.
ELECTRA.
Run along inside.
Even if you begged me, I'd not listen to you.
It's insane to ask for what's impossible to get.
CHRYSOTHEMIS.
If you think you're wise, then so be it.
Your heart will soon be sore that you did not hear my words.

(CHRYSOTHEMIS exits.)

CHORUS.
Consider the birds of the air.
In their fragile nest they sustain
Those who gave them life and pleasure.
So should we pay to those of our name
That debt, that bond of nature.
As God is just, guardian of all laws,
No mortal escapes punishment.
The day of judgment dawns.
O voice that's truly heaven sent,
Tell this to the dead below,

Tell Agamemnon this great sorrow,
His house is standing desolate.
The ties of blood are torn.
Where once was love there now is hatred.
Alone, Electra mourns.
She weeps for her poor father
Like a bird who's lost its child.
She looks upon his killers,
And her heart is driven wild.
Where shall you find on this earth
A woman to match her worth?
The wisest, best of daughters,
Electra mourns alone.
She waits for her glory till stone
Turns to water.
May I see you in that glory,
May I see your blood restored.
Your fate will change, it will come good,
You feared God's law, and you feared God.

(ORESTES and PYLADES enter.)

    ORESTES.
Tell me, women, are we on the right road to our destination?
    CHORUS.
What are you looking for—why are you here?
    ORESTES.
I've been looking a long time for the home of Aegisthus.
    CHORUS.
You've come the right way—it's here.
    ORESTES.
Could you tell them we have arrived?
They have long been waiting for us.
    CHORUS.
This young woman should do that—she's related to them.

ORESTES.
Lady, tell them some Phocians are looking for Aegisthus.
ELECTRA.
Don't tell me you've come with proof positive of the story
          we've heard.
ORESTES.
What story?
I was told to bring news about Orestes.

ELECTRA.
What news?
I'm shaking with fear.
ORESTES
He's dead.
This small urn - it contains all that is left of him.
Are you weeping for Orestes?
This is his dust.
ELECTRA.
If those are his ashes, give me that to hold.
I'll weep for that dust, and for myself.
I'll weep for my whole family.
ORESTES.
Give this to her.
She means no harm to it.
She's a friend to him, or one of his family.
ELECTRA.
Orestes, the man I loved most,
This is all that is left of you.
I sent you away from here, full of hope,
But your return has emptied all hope from me.
Now you are nothing,
And I hold you in my hands,
But the day you left, you were the light of day.
I wish I had died before I saved you from death.
I sent you into a foreign land.
You could have fallen here beside your father,

You could have lain with him in his grave.
But you died in exile, far from home, from your sister.
It was a sad death.
I was not there.
I could not wash your lovely corpse with my hands.
I could not snatch your lovely bones from the pyre.
Strangers' hands buried you.
You come back to me as dust, a handful of dust.
I nursed you as a baby, I didn't mind the bother,
You were never your mother's child, you were mine.
No one else in that house cared for you but me.
You called me sister—sister you called me.
All vanished in a day, dead with your death.
The wind's come and blown everything away.
Your father's dead, and I'm dead, and you're lost.
Those who stand against us laugh.
Your mother, who is not mother, is mad with joy.
Her crimes, I know, you would have put a stop to them.
But fate is cruel, your fate and mine.
It does not bring me your beautiful face.
No, it delivers cold ash and useless shadow.
Pain—
Pain—
Pain—
Pain—
Pain—
You have destroyed me, my loved, loved brother,
Yes, you have destroyed me.
Take me with you.
I am nothing, let me turn into nothing with you.
We live as one together on this earth.
Now I want to die with you in the grave.
For the dead do not mourn, they do not mourn.
    CHORUS.
Electra, child, you are mortal,
Your father and Orestes too—mortal.

Death comes to us all.
We have to face it.
    ORESTES.
What can I say?
I cannot speak, but I can no longer hold my tongue.
    ELECTRA.
Why do you say that—what's wrong with you?
    ORESTES.
Am I looking at the great woman, Electra?
    ELECTRA.
That is me, and I'm a sorry sight.
    ORESTES.
Yours is a pitiful story. So pitiful.
    ELECTRA.
Sir, your pity is not for me, surely.
    ORESTES.
Your beauty has been broken and wickedly disfigured.
    ELECTRA.
Yes, sir, I am the woman your words describe.
    ORESTES.
They stopped you from marrying—they've sentenced you to
        misery.
    ELECTRA.
Stranger, why do you look at me and lament?
    ORESTES.
I've known so little of my own sorrow.
    ELECTRA.
What have I said to tell you that?
    ORESTES.
Because you are marked by many sorrows.
    ELECTRA.
You see only half of them.
    ORESTES.
What worse pain could there be than this?
    ELECTRA.
To live with murderers.

ORESTES.
Whose murderers?
What evil are you whispering about?
ELECTRA.
My father's, and I am their slave.
ORESTES.
Who demands this?
ELECTRA.
My mother, who is mother only in name.
ORESTES.
What does she do?
Is she violent, does she deprive you—
ELECTRA.
She is violent—she deprives me—
ORESTES.
Is there no one to help you prevent it?
ELECTRA.
There was one—you've shown me his ashes.
ORESTES.
Poor girl, for a long time I've looked at you with pity.
ELECTRA.
You are the first who has ever pitied me.
ORESTES.
I am the first to know your pain is my pain.
ELECTRA.
Who are you—some relative from far away?
ORESTES.
If these women are on our side, I can tell you.
ELECTRA.
They're with us, you can trust them.
ORESTES.
Give me back that urn, and I'll tell you everything.
ELECTRA.
Please, stranger, don't ask me to do that.
ORESTES.
Do as I say, you won't regret it.

ELECTRA.
Don't take what I love most in this life.
ORESTES.
I won't let you keep it.
ELECTRA.
My loved Orestes, I cannot even bury you.
ORESTES.
Be quiet—you have no reason to weep.
ELECTRA.
No reason to weep—my brother's dead!
ORESTES.
You have not right to call him that.
ELECTRA.
Do you refuse to let me respect the dead?
ORESTES.
You are refused nothing, but this doesn't belong to you.
ELECTRA.
It does, if this is my brother's body.
ORESTES.
It is not him. It is not Orestes.
ELECTRA.
Then where is his grave?
ORESTES.
There is none—we don't bury the living.
ELECTRA.
Son, what are you saying?
ORESTES.
All I say is true.
ELECTRA.
Is the man alive?
ORESTES.
Alive as I am.
ELECTRA.
Orestes—is it you?
ORESTES.
My father's signet ring—am I telling the truth?

(ELECTRA gives a cry of joy, matched by ORESTES.)

ELECTRA.
Do I hear your voice again?
ORESTES.
My voice—none other.
ELECTRA.
Do I hold you in my arms?
ORESTES.
Hold me there for ever.
ELECTRA.
Dear woman, dear friend, look—it's Orestes.
We thought him dead—know now he's alive.
CHORUS.
Daughter, we see him and we're crying for your good fortune.
ELECTRA.
My darling, darling son, you've come home.
You're here, you've arrived, you've seen those you love.
ORESTES.
I'm here but sssh—wait.
ELECTRA.
What's wrong?
ORESTES.
It's best to keep quiet in case anyone in there should hear.
ELECTRA.
I swear by the Virgin I fear no one in that house.
Those women are good for nothing.
They're a waste of space on this earth.
ORESTES.
Women can fight as well.
You know that from experience.
ELECTRA.
Oh, you've brought back the old sorrow,
Never hide it—nothing can heal it—never forget it.
ORESTES.
I know that as well.

But the hour is coming.
We'll remember what they did.
    ELECTRA.
I could tell what they did till the end of time.
My lips have been long sealed, now they're free.
    ORESTES.
True, but mind how freely you speak.
    ELECTRA.
Why?
    ORESTES.
Don't say too much until the time is right.
    ELECTRA.
Who could be silent? Who could say nothing?
I've seen you.
I never thought—I gave up hope.
    ORESTES.
You see me here because the gods told me to come now.
    ELECTRA.
If the gods brought you here, this is their greatest gift.
And in your being here, I see the hand of heaven.
    ORESTES.
I don't want to limit your happiness, but it's too great—
You're frightening me.
    ELECTRA.
I welcome you back with open arms, you're here,
You've seen how I was suffering, do not—
    ORESTES.
Do not do what?
    ELECTRA.
Take the light of day from me.
I find it in your face.
    ORESTES.
Then find it there and in no other.
    ELECTRA.
Do you allow me?

ORESTES.
I do.
ELECTRA.
Dear women, I've heard a voice I'd lost all hope of hearing.
How could I be silent and not give one cry of joy?
I have you now.
I see your face, I'll see it for ever.
I'll never forget.
ORESTES.
Say no more now.
I know how vile our mother is.
I know Aegisthus wastes our father's wealth.
This is not the time for these stories.
Tell me instead what we need to do.
Do we reveal ourselves, or do we lie in wait?
How do we wipe the smiles off our enemies' faces?
When we go inside,
Wipe the smile off your face.
Weep as if the tragic story were true.
When the battle's won, we'll have time to laugh.
ELECTRA.
Brother, I'll do everything to please you.
I would not harm you, even if it were to help myself.
The gods are on our side, I'll serve them.
You know how things stand here.
Aegisthus is not at home, our mother is in the house.
Don't worry, she won't see a smile on my face.
My hatred of her is too deep.
Since you've come back I've been weeping, weeping for joy.
On the one day I've seen you dead and alive.
How could I not weep?
It is a miracle.
If my father came back from the dead, I'd believe it.
Fate has guided you, so I'll do as you bid.
If I'd been left alone, I'd have done one of two things—
Live or die like a brave woman.

ORESTES.
Be quiet—I hear someone coming from the house.

(The old SERVANT enters.)

SERVANT.
Are you two complete fools?
Are you tired of living?
Have you not enough sense to see the danger you're
          steeped in?
I have been watching you, and it's just as well.
Those inside would have guessed what plot you're
          hatching.
As it is, I've taken care to prevent them doing so.
You've had your fill of welcomes and words of joy.
Get inside now.
Any more delay does us no good—make an end to this.
          ORESTES.
When I go in, how shall I find things?
          SERVANT.
Everything's well—there's no chance they'll know you.
          ORESTES.
You've told them I'm dead?
          SERVANT.
Here you're dead and in the grave.
          ORESTES.
Are they pleased at that—what do they say?
          SERVANT.
I'll tell you all when you've settled this business.
Inside all is as well, or as wicked, as you'd expect.
          ELECTRA.
Tell me, who is this, brother?
          ORESTES.
Do you not see?
          ELECTRA.
I have never set eyes on him.

ORESTES.

Do you not know the man into whose hands you once put me?

ELECTRA.

What are you saying—what man?

ORESTES.

The man you trusted to carry me to Phocis.

ELECTRA.

This is the only one who stayed loyal to my murdered father?

ORESTES.

That's the man—let that be enough, ask no more questions.

ELECTRA.

This is a great day.

The one good man in Agamemnon's house—how have you
        come here?

Are you the man who saved us both from so many troubles?

I bless your hands, I bless your feet.

How could you be here so long without my knowing you?

Your news killed me, but the truth's brought me back to life.

I greet you as a father, for I think you are a father.

In one day I have hated and loved you like no other man.

SERVANT.

That's enough for now.

There will be plenty of time to tell all, Electra.

But don't stand here—it's time to act, you two men.

Clytemnestra is alone,

There is no man inside.

If you hold back now, you'll face an army soon.

ORESTES.

No more time for words, Pylades,

Time to get inside.

If you hold back now, you'll face an army soon.

First we'll pray to the gods that guard
  my father's house.

(ORESTES, PYLADES and the SERVANT enter the palace.
ELECTRA prays to the statue of Apollo.)

ELECTRA.
Lord Apollo. Hear their prayer—hear mine also.
I've stood before you often.
I made you offerings form what little I possessed.
Now I ask, Lord Apollo, with all I have,
I fall before you, I implore you,
Let our work prosper,
Show to the godless how the gods reward evil.
    CHORUS.
The God of War advances,
Breathing blood and vengeance.
The hounds are on the trail,
The sinners wait within.
My mind can see it all,
There's no escaping death.
The champion of the dead,
He's entered the house,
Ancestral hall of kings.
His sword is smelling blood.
    ELECTRA.
Good women, say nothing, but the men will soon finish
        the work.
    CHORUS.
What are they doing?
    ELECTRA.
They stand by her as she prepares the urn for burial.
    CHORUS.
Why have you rushed out?
    ELECTRA.
To watch in case Aegisthus surprises us.

(CLYTEMNESTRA cries from within the palace.)

CLYTEMNESTRA.
Is there none to help me?
Are you all killers?
    ELECTRA.
Do you hear, friends—someone inside is crying out.
    CHORUS.
I've heard that dreadful cry—it frightens me.
    CLYTEMNESTRA.
Aegisthus, where are you?
    ELECTRA.
Listen—another cry.
    CLYTEMNESTRA.
Son—son—have mercy on your mother.
    ELECTRA.
You had none for him nor the man who fathered him.
    CHORUS.
My unhappy city, this unhappy house,
A curse was placed upon you.
Now it's being lifted.
    CLYTEMNESTRA.
You have struck me.
    ELECTRA.
If you can, strike her again.
    CLYTEMNESTRA.
God help me—God help me.
    ELECTRA.
I wish Aegisthus were with you.
    CHORUS.
The curse has worked.
The dead live again,
Draining the blood of the living.

(ORESTES and PYLADES enter from the palace.)

CHORUS.
Look—their hands are stained,
And I do not condemn them.
ELECTRA.
How have you fared, Orestes?
ORESTES.
I have done well, if Apollo spoke the truth.
ELECTRA.
Is that foul woman dead?
ORESTES.
Your mother will no longer displease you.
CHORUS.
Stop—I see Aegisthus coming.
ELECTRA.
Back into the house.
ORESTES.
Where do you see him?
ELECTRA.
Coming down the street.
He's smiling.
He is ours.
CHORUS.
Hurry into the palace.
You've done half your work well.
Now, finish it perfectly.
ORESTES.
We will—don't worry.
ELECTRA.
Get to where you're going.
ORESTES.
I'm on my way.
ELECTRA.
Leave matters here to me.

(ORESTES and PYLADES exit.)

CHORUS.
Speak gently to him.
Let him walk blindly into the trap of Justice.

(AEGISTHUS enters.)

AEGISTHUS.
Can any tell me where the Phocian strangers are?
I've heard they say Orestes died falling from a chariot.
You—I'm asking you—you had enough to say before.
You have most to lose by this, so you should know.
     ELECTRA.
Of course I know.
I should know what's happened to those I love most.
     AEGISTHUS.
Where are they—tell me immediately.
     ELECTRA.
Inside—they've warmed the heart of their hostess.
     AEGISTHUS.
Do they truly say he was dead?
     ELECTRA.
They did—they even showed us the dead man.
     AEGISTHUS.
May I see the body too—to make sure?
     ELECTRA.
You may, but it's an ugly sight.
     AEGISTHUS.
For once, your words please me.
     ELECTRA.
Stay pleased, if you've reason to be.
     AEGISTHUS.
Throw open the door.
Let all Mycenae and Argos see.
If you had hopes in this man, he is dead.
Now accept my rule—or face the dire consequences.

ELECTRA.
I've learnt my lesson.
Time's taught me to side with the strong.

*(The doors open. There is a shrouded corpse with ORESTES
and PYLADES beside it.)*

AEGISTHUS.
Zeus, this man was laid low by the angry gods.
If that anger was justified, let me not say so.
Remove the covering from that face.
I must mourn for my relation.
ORESTES.
Remove it yourself.
You must look at this and speak kind words.
AEGISTHUS.
Well said, I will.
Call Clytemnestra, if she is in the house.
ORESTES.
She is beside you—look.
(AEGISTHUS lifts the covering. He starts in horror.)
Why are you frightened?
Don't you recognize the face?
AEGISTHUS.
Who has set the trap that I've fallen into?
ORESTES.
Do you know you have been talking to the dead?
AEGISTHUS.
Orestes—I understand—it's you.
ORESTES.
You are so deep, and yet so long deceived.
AEGISTHUS.
You will kill me.
Let me say one thing—

ELECTRA.
Let him say nothing, brother, not one word.
He is doomed and let him die now.
Kill him, give his corpse to whoever will bury him.
Get him out of our sight.
Then and only then will I be rid of the wrongs he has done.
    ORESTES.
Get inside.
Words won't save you—I want your life.
    AEGISTHUS.
Why do you force me into the house?
If what you're doing is right, why do it in darkness?
Why not kill me here?
    ORESTES.
Give me no orders—get inside.
    AEGISTHUS.
Is this house forever cursed?
Shall there be killing after killing for ever?
    ORESTES.
There shall be yours—that much I can see clearly.
    AEGISTHUS.
Then you see more than your father ever did.
    ORESTES.
Your words are wasting my time.
Get inside.
    AEGISTHUS.
You lead the way.
    ORESTES.
You go first.
    AEGISTHUS.
In case I run away?
    ORESTES.
No—in case you choose where to die.
I want you to taste the bitterness of death.
Your sentence is swift and severe.

(AEGISTHUS exits, followed by ORESTES and PYLADES.)

CHORUS.
Children of Atreus,
Your suffering has ended.
You have won freedom.
The deed is done.

END OF PLAY

Set Drawing
ELECTRA

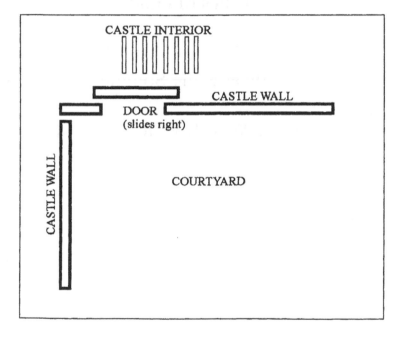

Also By
Frank McGuinness

Gates of Gold

Observe the Sons of Ulster Marching Towards the Somme

Someone Who'll Watch Over Me

OTHER TITLES AVAILABLE FROM SAMUEL FRENCH

SOMEONE WHO'LL WATCH OVER ME
Frank McGuinness

Drama / 3m/ Interior

An American doctor and an Irish journalist are being held captive by terrorists in Beirut. They exercise and they argue, supportive in their mutual determination to survive. They are joined by an English academic. The three display their national biases and prejudices, which are intensified in the cramped confines of their cell. As time passes, resentments and recriminations give way to an acknowledgment of their characters, strengths and weaknesses. They learn that humor is their surest weapon against their captors and the safest armor to protect themselves. They shoot imaginary films, they throw a big party for each other, they play a fantastical game of tennis, they laugh at and with each other, and they learn to lament what was lost in their lives before captivity. Each comes to know himself through listening to the stories, sorrows and joys of the others. At the end of the play, they are capable of standing together and alone.

"Brings its own light touch to grim matters."
–The New York Times

"A beautiful play."
–The New Yorker

SAMUEL FRENCH STAFF

Nate Collins
President

Ken Dingledine
Director of Operations,
Vice President

Bruce Lazarus
Executive Director,
General Counsel

Rita Maté
Director of Finance

ACCOUNTING

Lori Thimsen | Director of Licensing Compliance
Nehal Kumar | Senior Accounting Associate
Josephine Messina | Accounts Payable
Helena Mezzina | Royalty Administration
Joe Garner | Royalty Administration
Jessica Zheng | Accounts Receivable
Andy Lian | Accounts Receivable
Zoe Qiu | Accounts Receivable
Charlie Sou | Accounting Associate
Joann Mannello | Orders Administrator

BUSINESS AFFAIRS

Lysna Marzani | Director of Business Affairs
Kathryn McCumber | Business Administrator

CUSTOMER SERVICE AND LICENSING

Brad Lohrenz | Director of Licensing Development
Fred Schnitzer | Business Development Manager
Laura Lindson | Licensing Services Manager
Kim Rogers | Professional Licensing Associate
Matthew Akers | Amateur Licensing Associate
Ashley Byrne | Amateur Licensing Associate
Glenn Halcomb | Amateur Licensing Associate
Derek Hassler | Amateur Licensing Associate
Jennifer Carter | Amateur Licensing Associate
Kelly McCready | Amateur Licensing Associate
Annette Storckman | Amateur Licensing Associate
Chris Lonstrup | Outgoing Information Specialist

EDITORIAL AND PUBLICATIONS

Amy Rose Marsh | Literary Manager
Ben Coleman | Editorial Associate
Gene Sweeney | Graphic Designer
David Geer | Publications Supervisor
Charlyn Brea | Publications Associate
Tyler Mullen | Publications Associate

MARKETING

Abbie Van Nostrand | Director of Corporate
Communications
Ryan Pointer | Marketing Manager
Courtney Kochuba | Marketing Associate

OPERATIONS

Joe Ferreira | Product Development Manager
Casey McLain | Operations Supervisor
Danielle Heckman | Office Coordinator, Reception

SAMUEL FRENCH BOOKSHOP (LOS ANGELES)

Joyce Mehess | Bookstore Manager
Cory DeLair | Bookstore Buyer
Jennifer Palumbo | Customer Service Associate
Sonya Wallace | Bookstore Associate
Tim Coultas | Bookstore Associate
Monté Patterson | Bookstore Associate
Robin Hushbeck | Bookstore Associate
Alfred Contreras | Shipping & Receiving

LONDON OFFICE

Felicity Barks | Rights & Contracts Associate
Steve Blacker | Bookshop Associate
David Bray | Customer Services Associate
Zena Choi | Professional Licensing Associate
Robert Cooke | Assistant Buyer
Stephanie Dawson | Amateur Licensing Associate
Simon Ellison | Retail Sales Manager
Jason Felix | Royalty Administration
Susan Griffiths | Amateur Licensing Associate
Robert Hamilton | Amateur Licensing Associate
Lucy Hume | Publications Manager
Nasir Khan | Management Accountant
Simon Magniti | Royalty Administration
Louise Mappley | Amateur Licensing Associate
James Nicolau | Despatch Associate
Martin Phillips | Librarian
Zubayed Rahman | Despatch Associate
Steve Sanderson | Royalty Administration Supervisor
Douglas Schatz | Acting Executive Director
Roger Sheppard | I.T. Manager
Geoffrey Skinner | Company Accountant
Peter Smith | Amateur Licensing Associate
Garry Spratley | Customer Service Manager
David Webster | UK Operations Director